THIS BOOK BELONGS TO

....

....

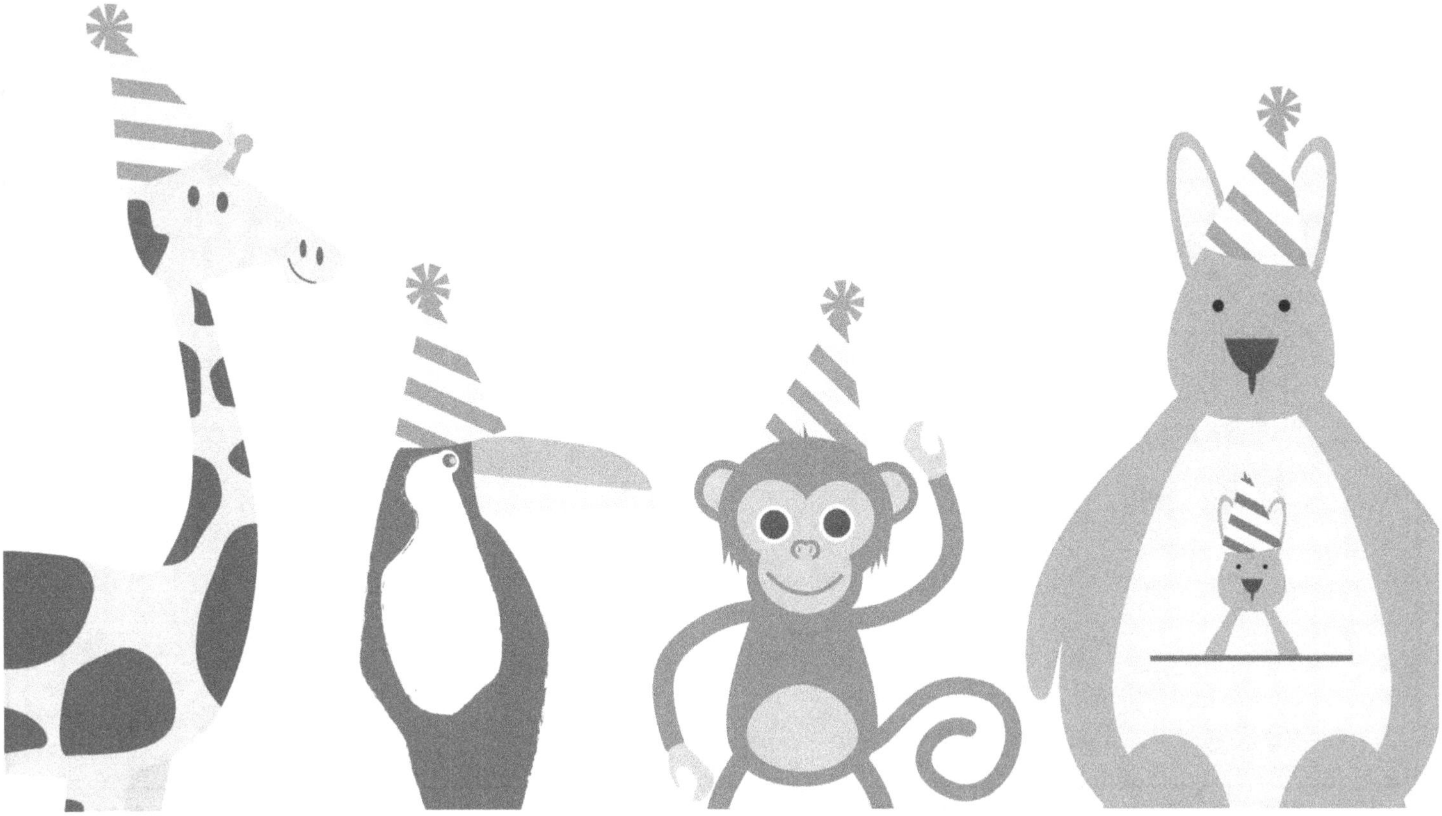

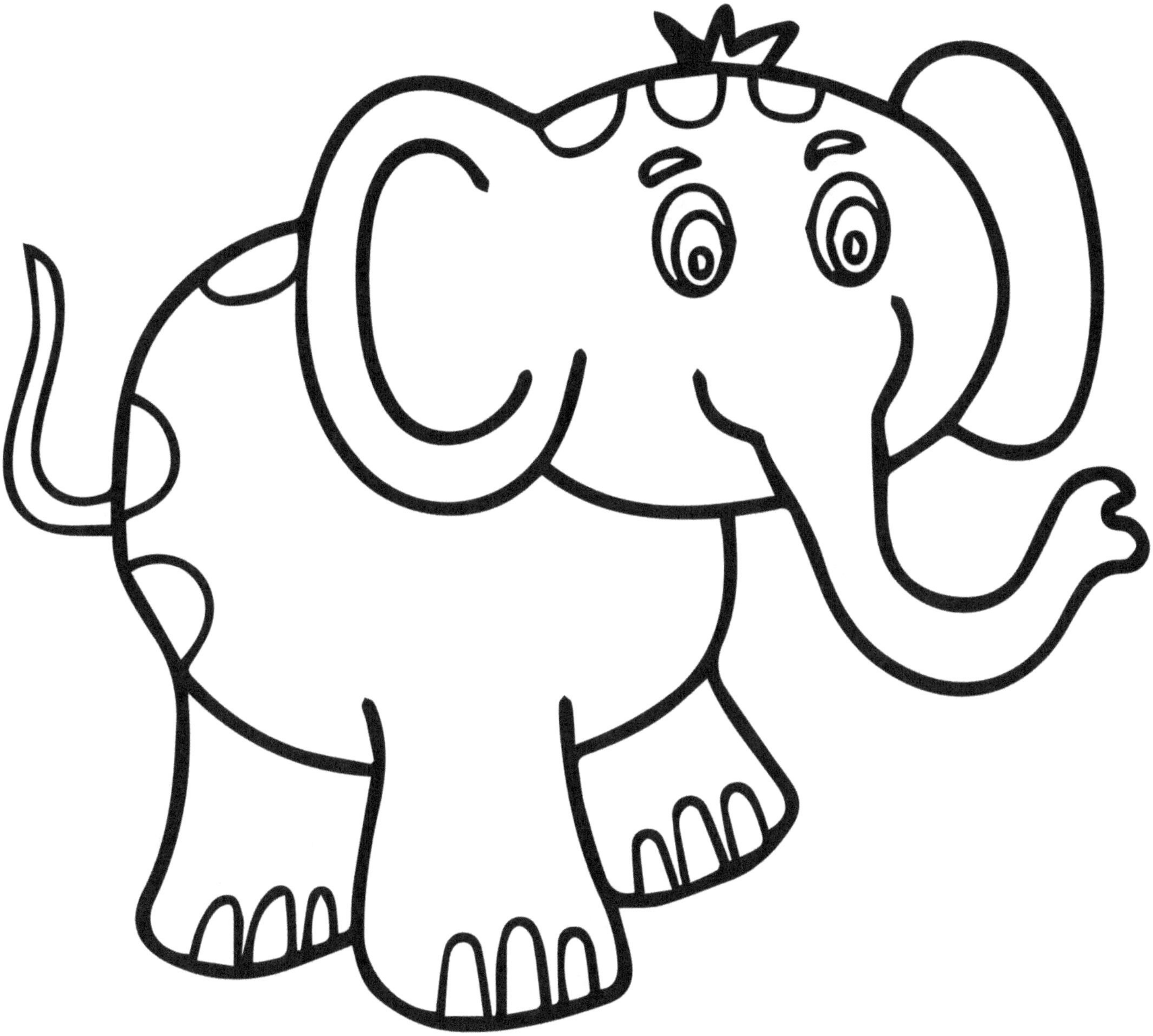

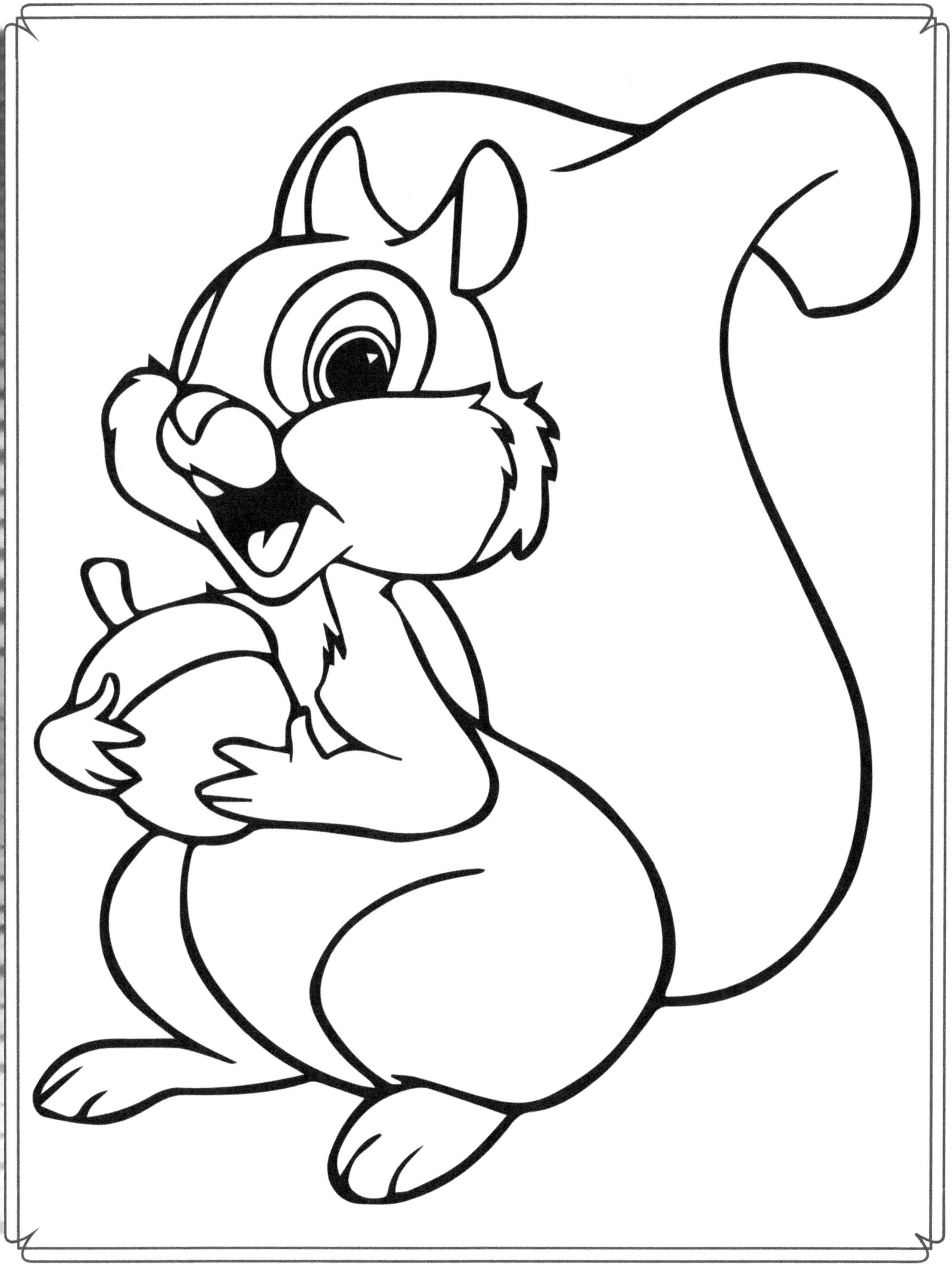

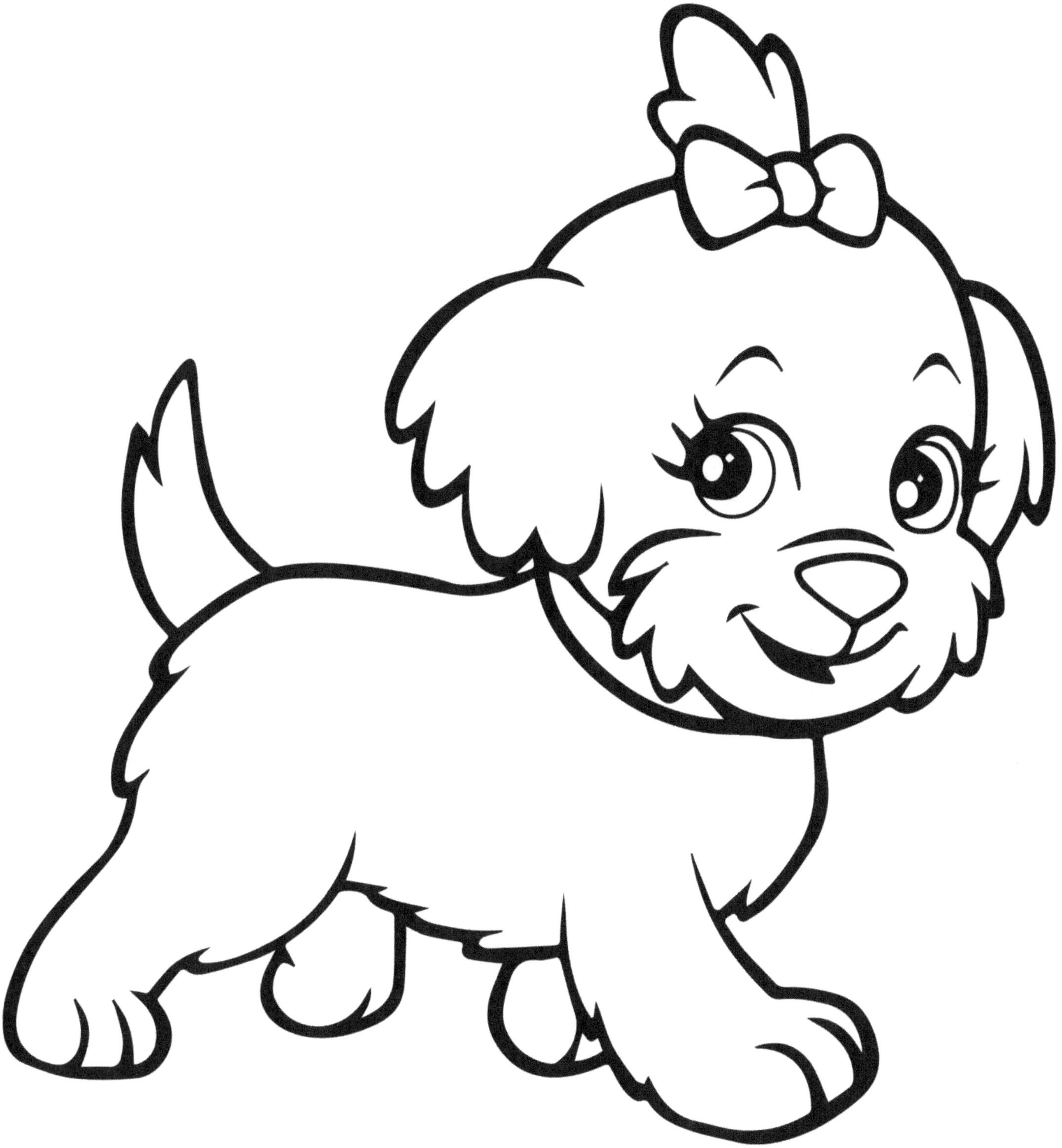

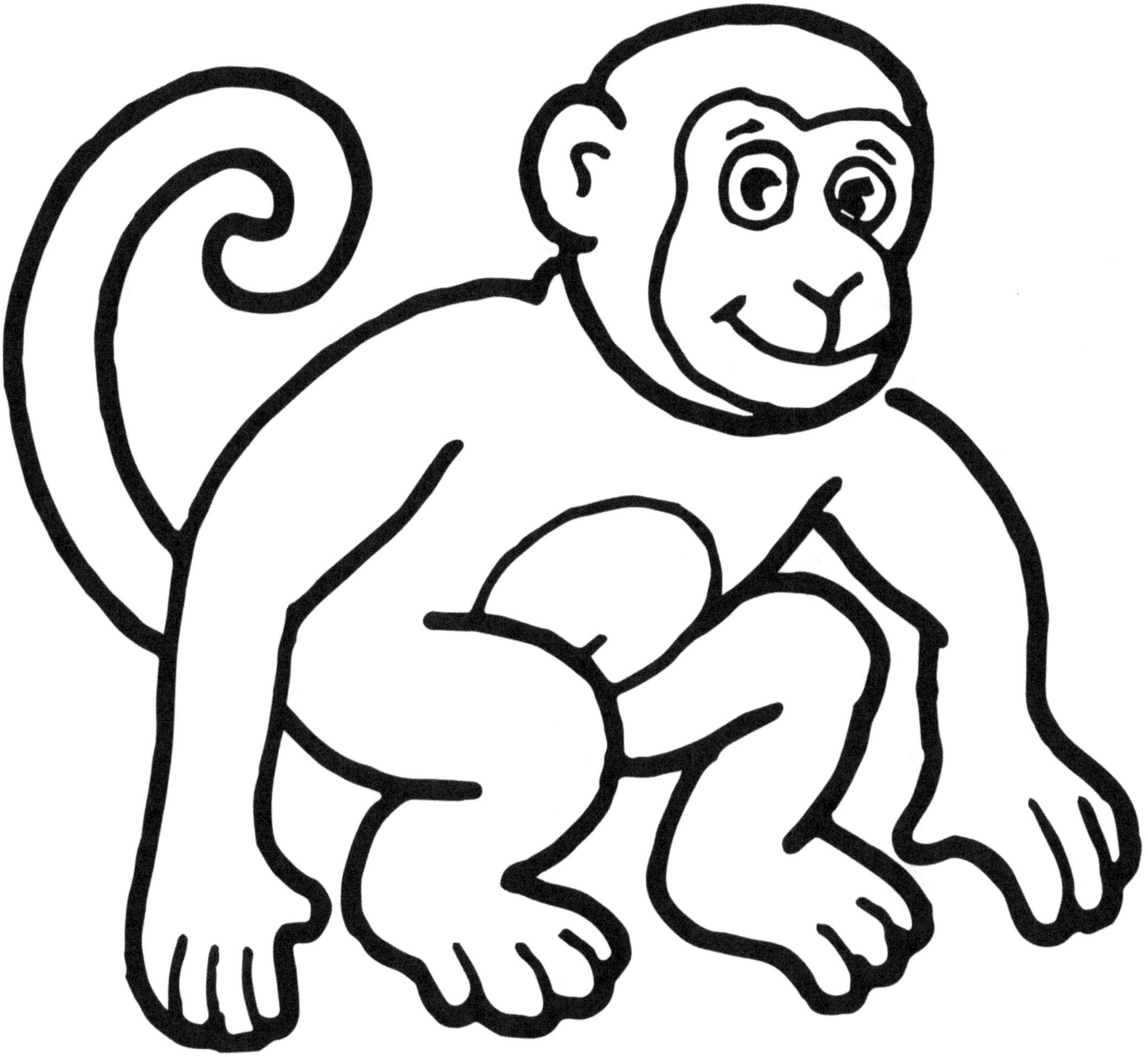

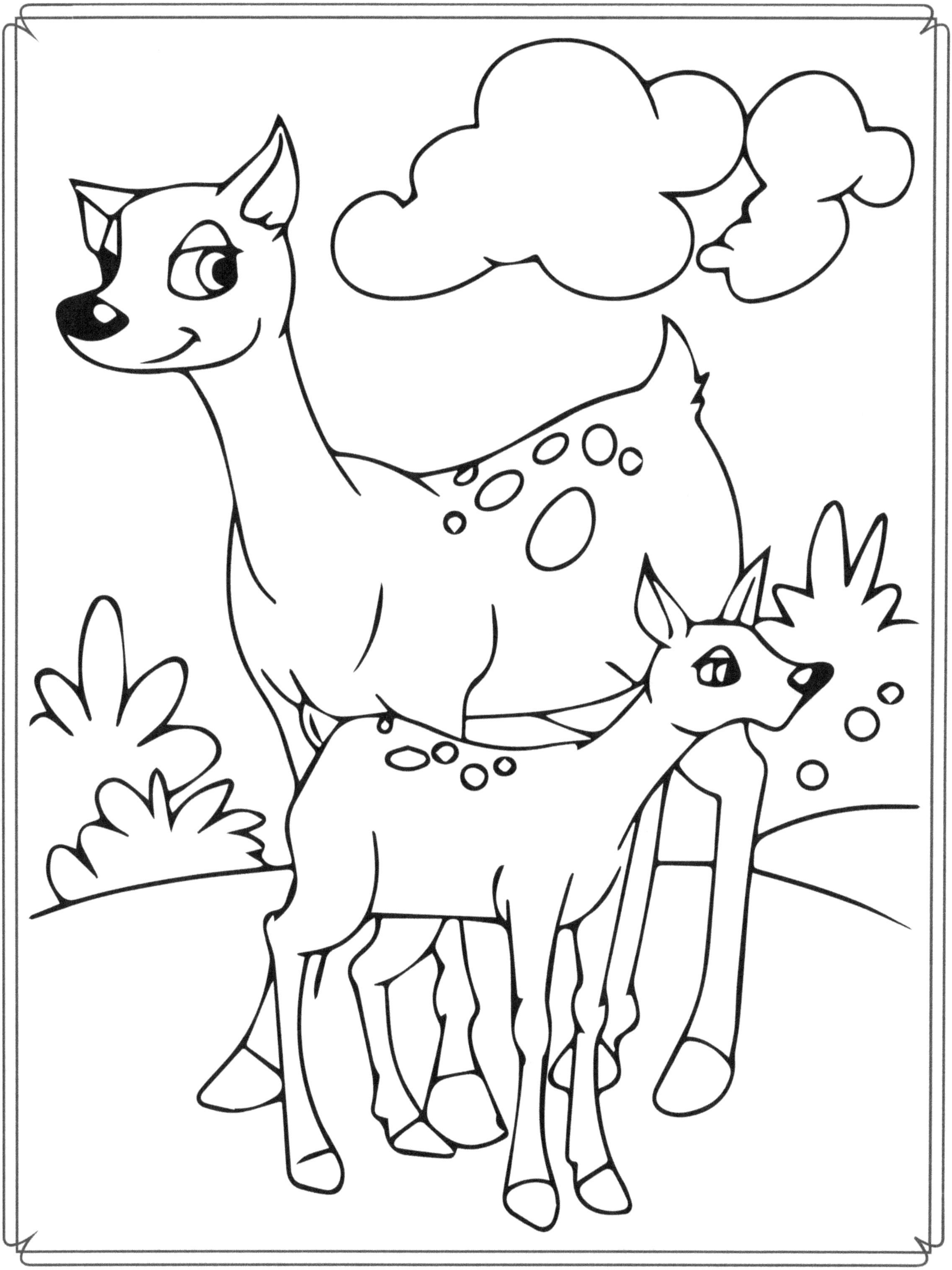

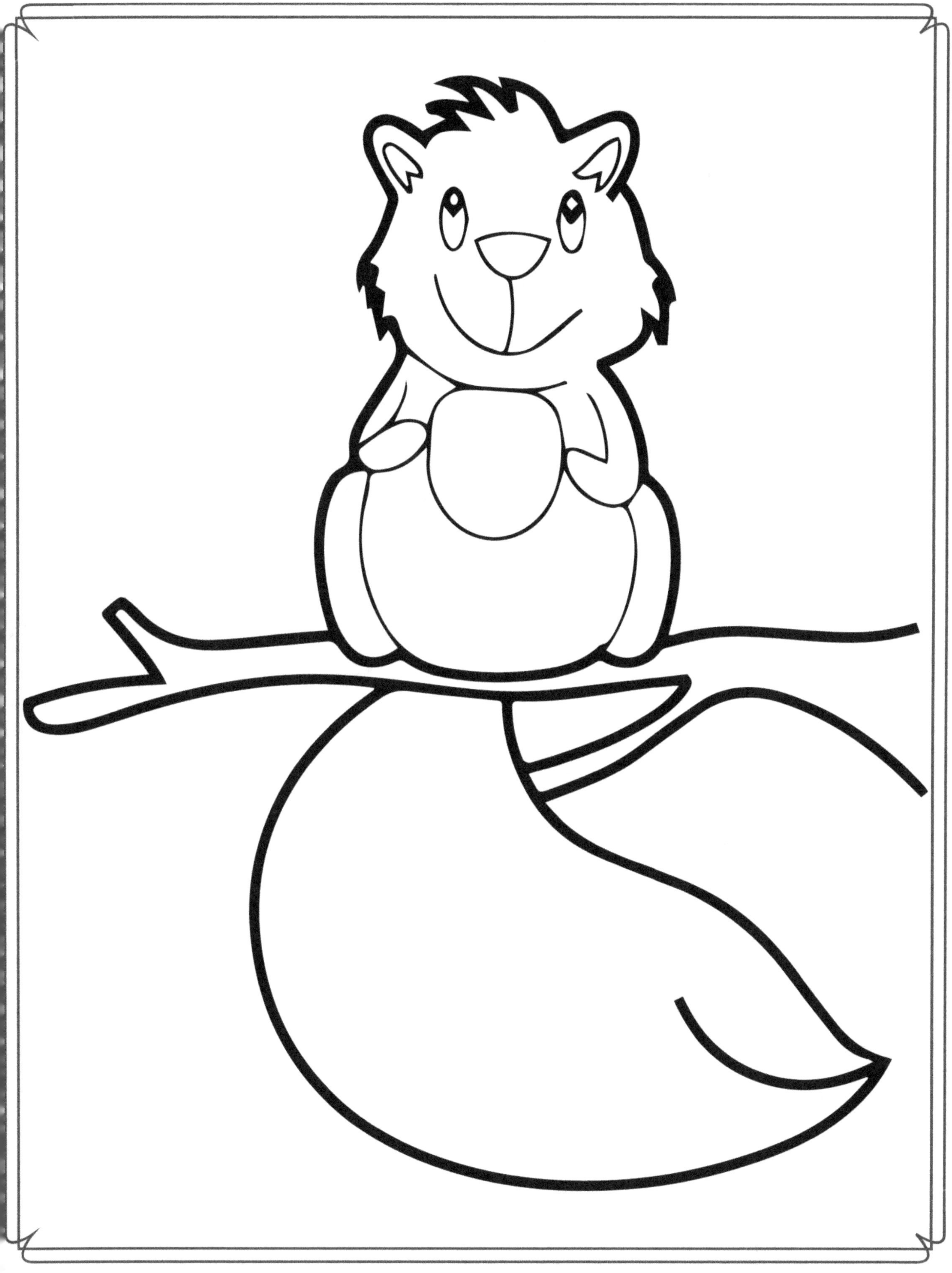

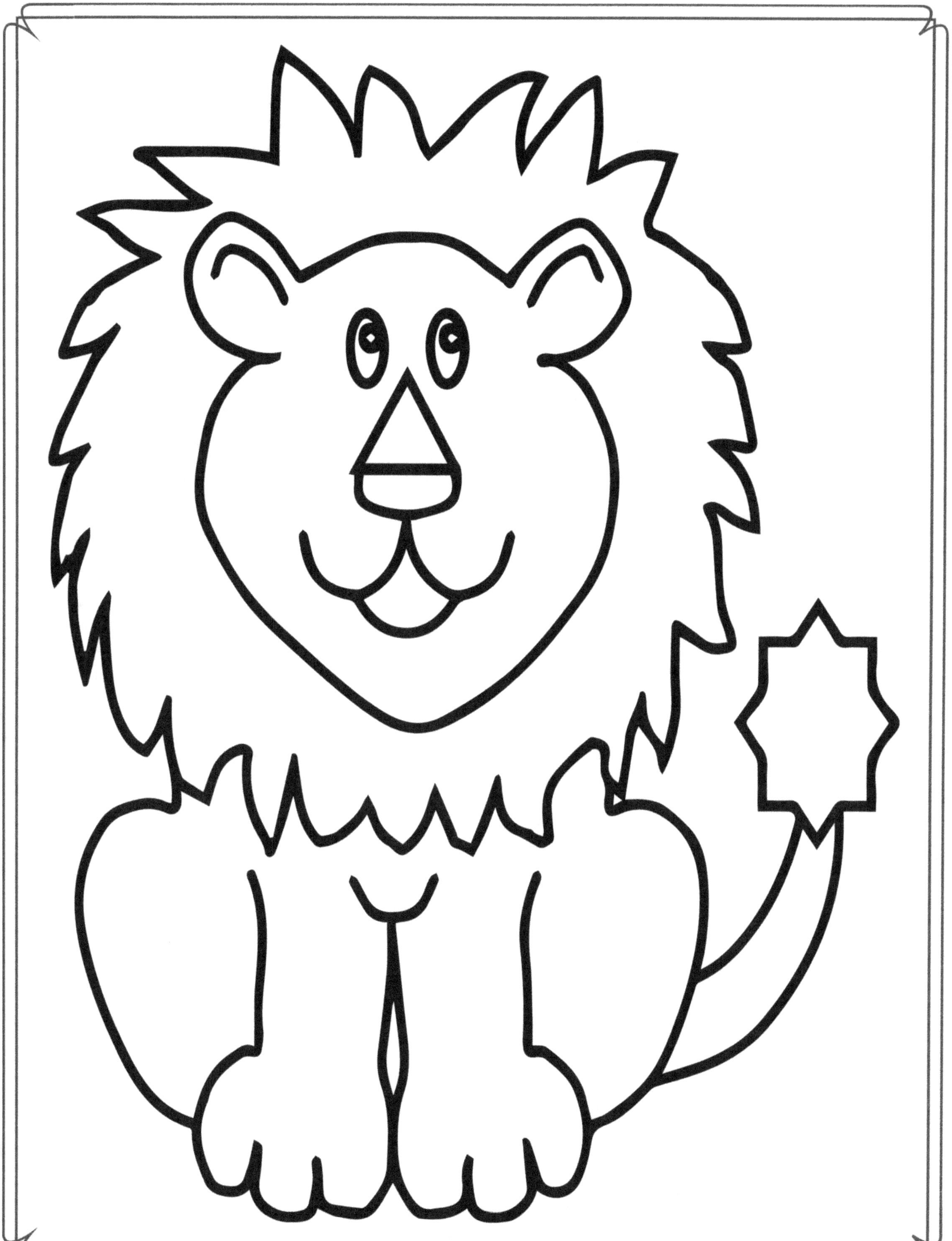

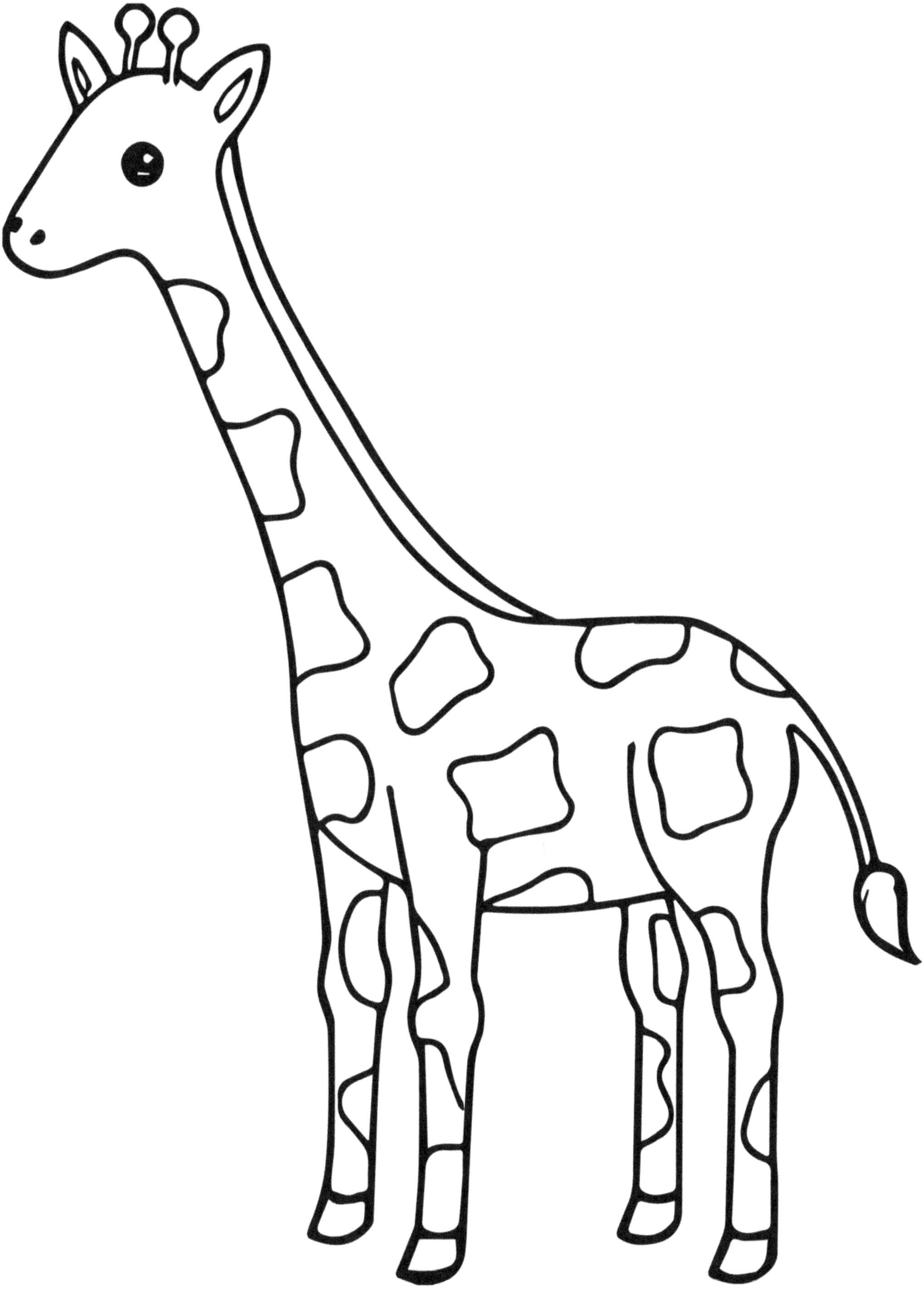

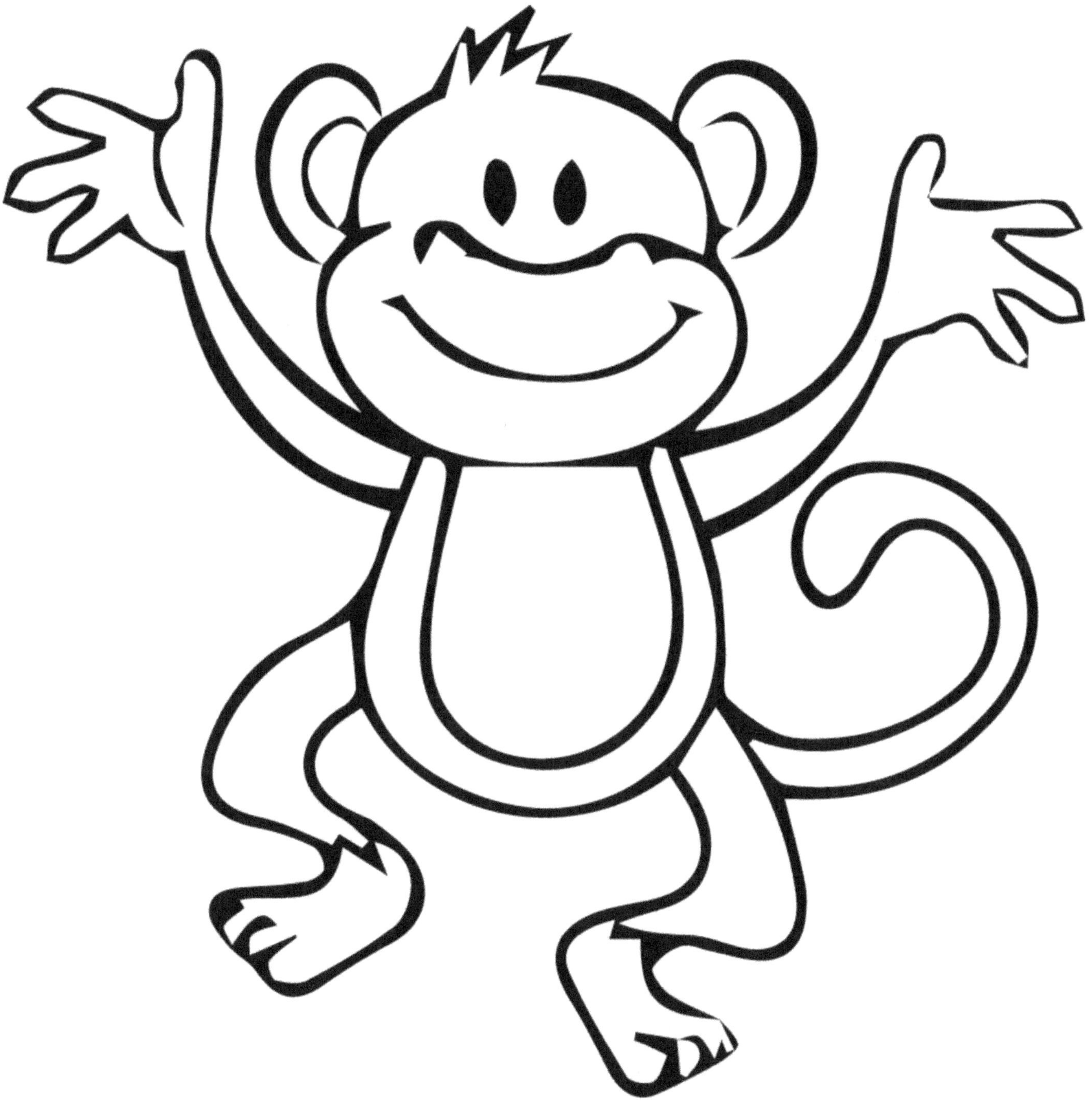

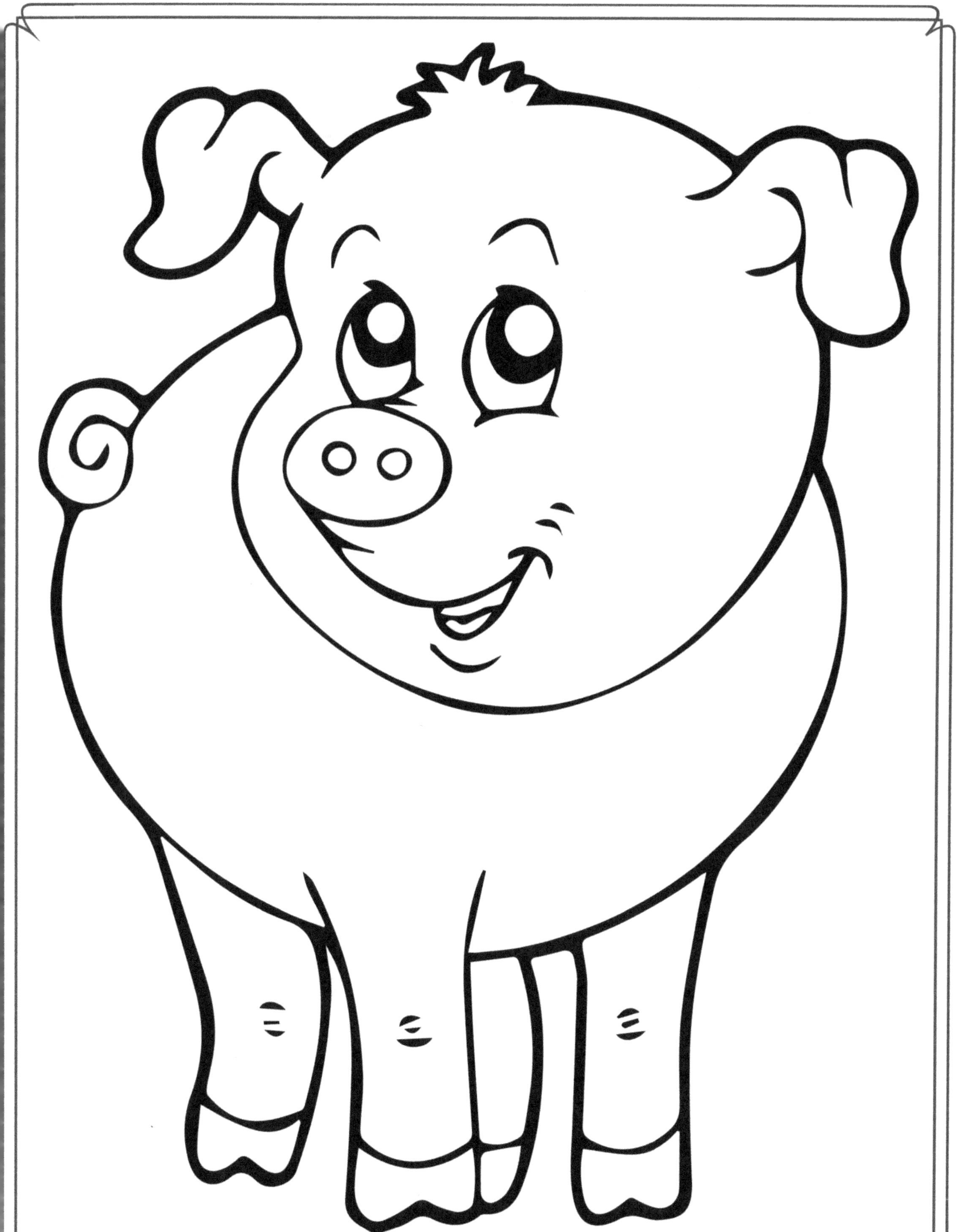

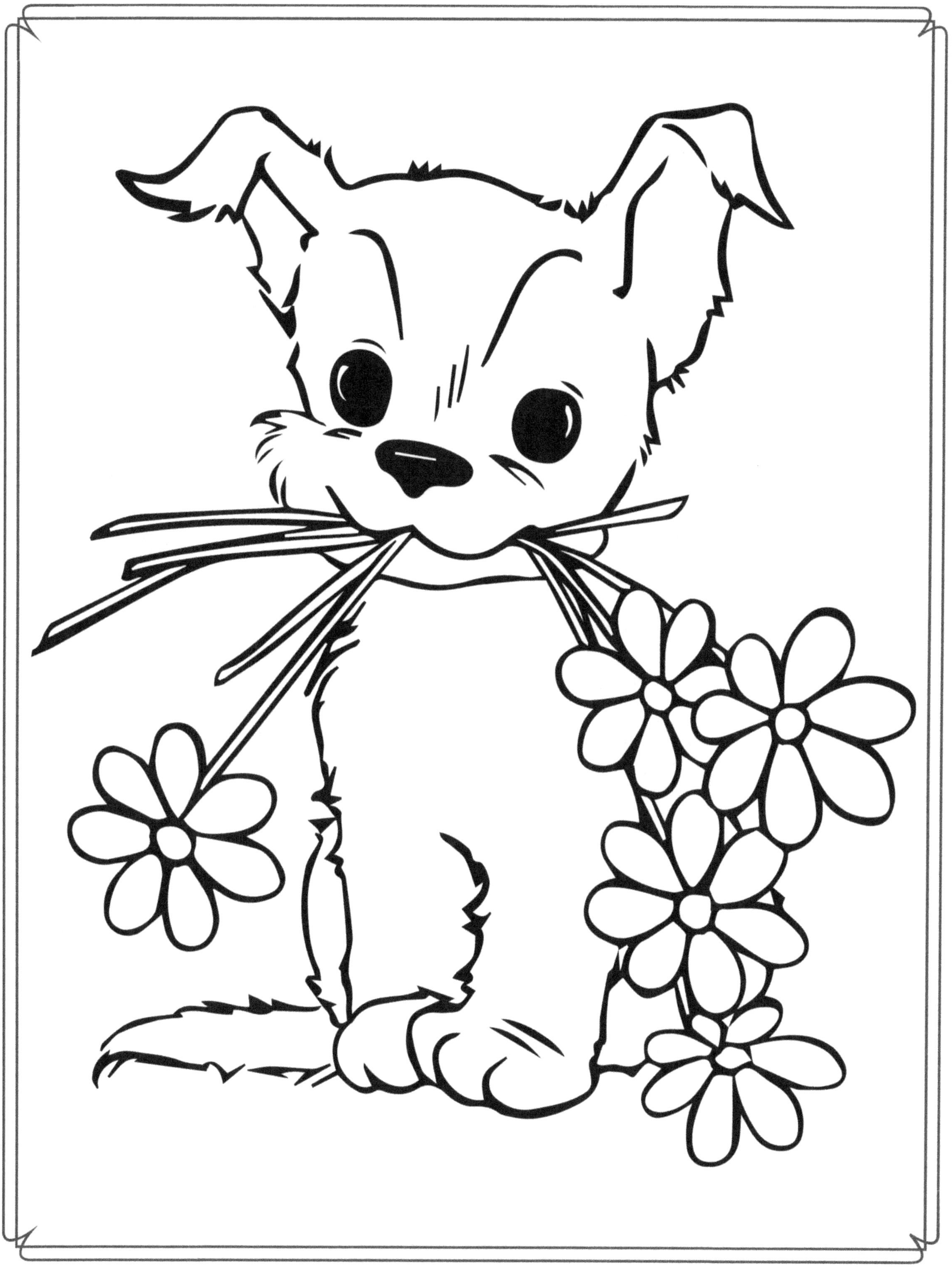

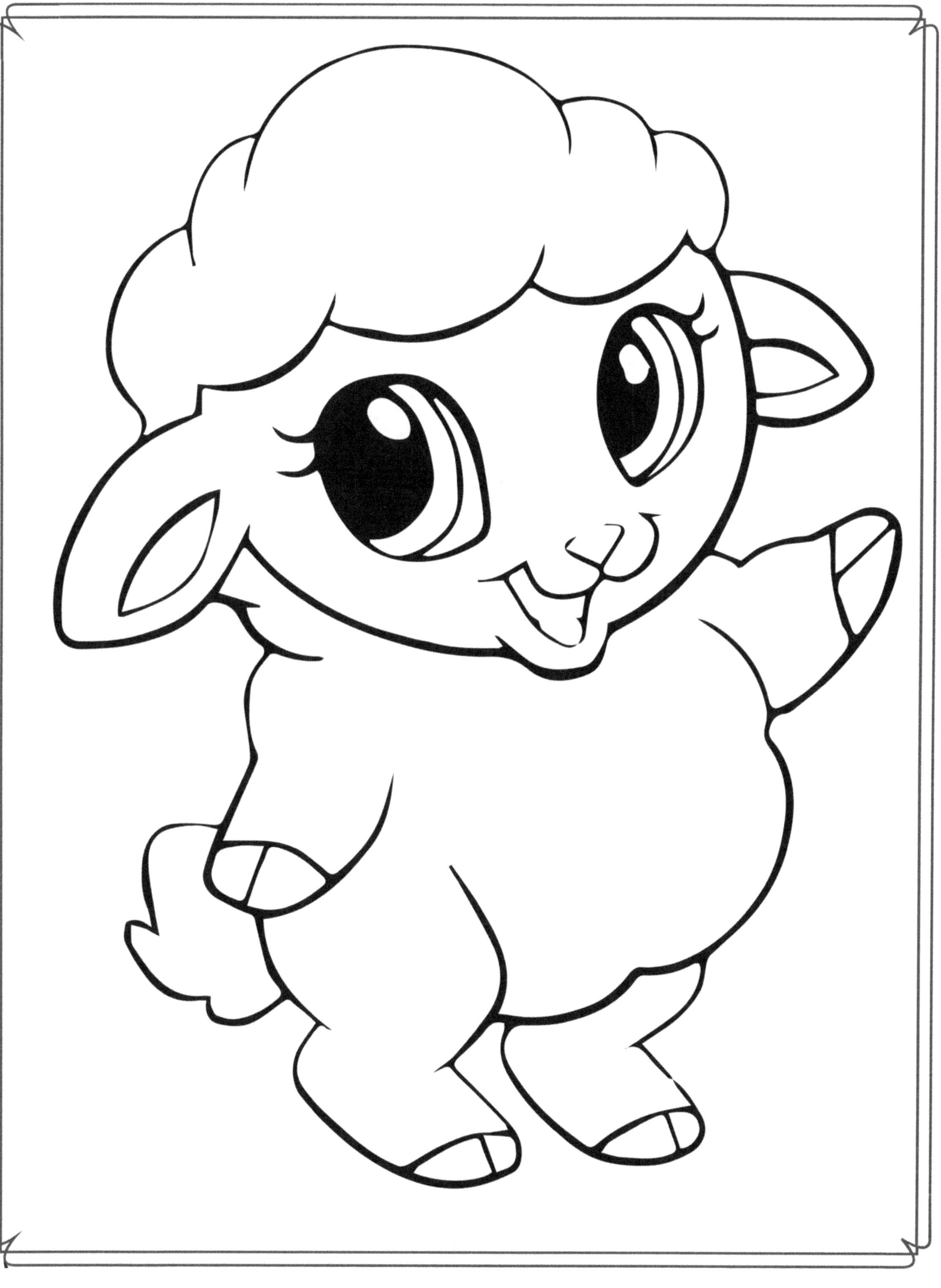

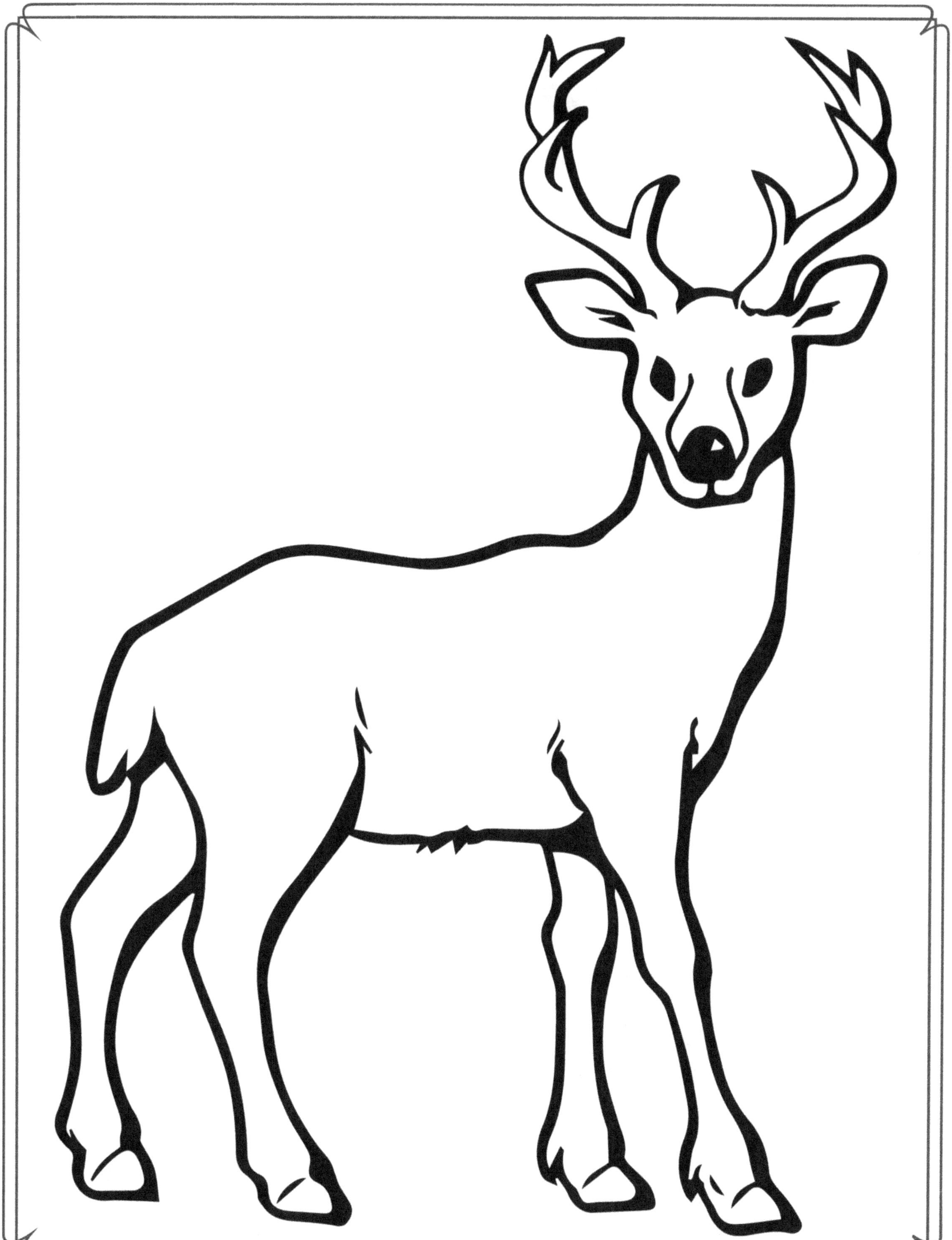

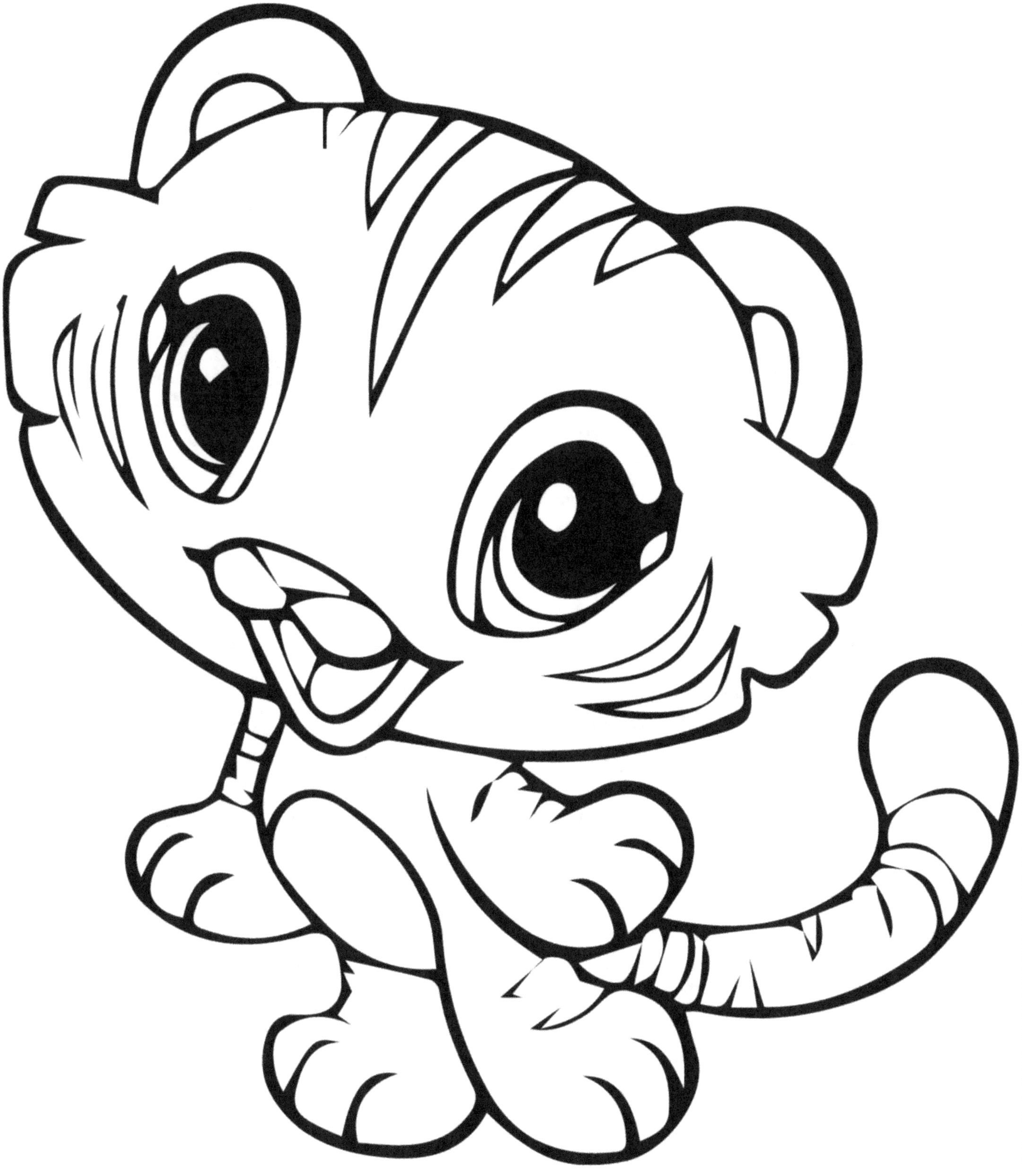

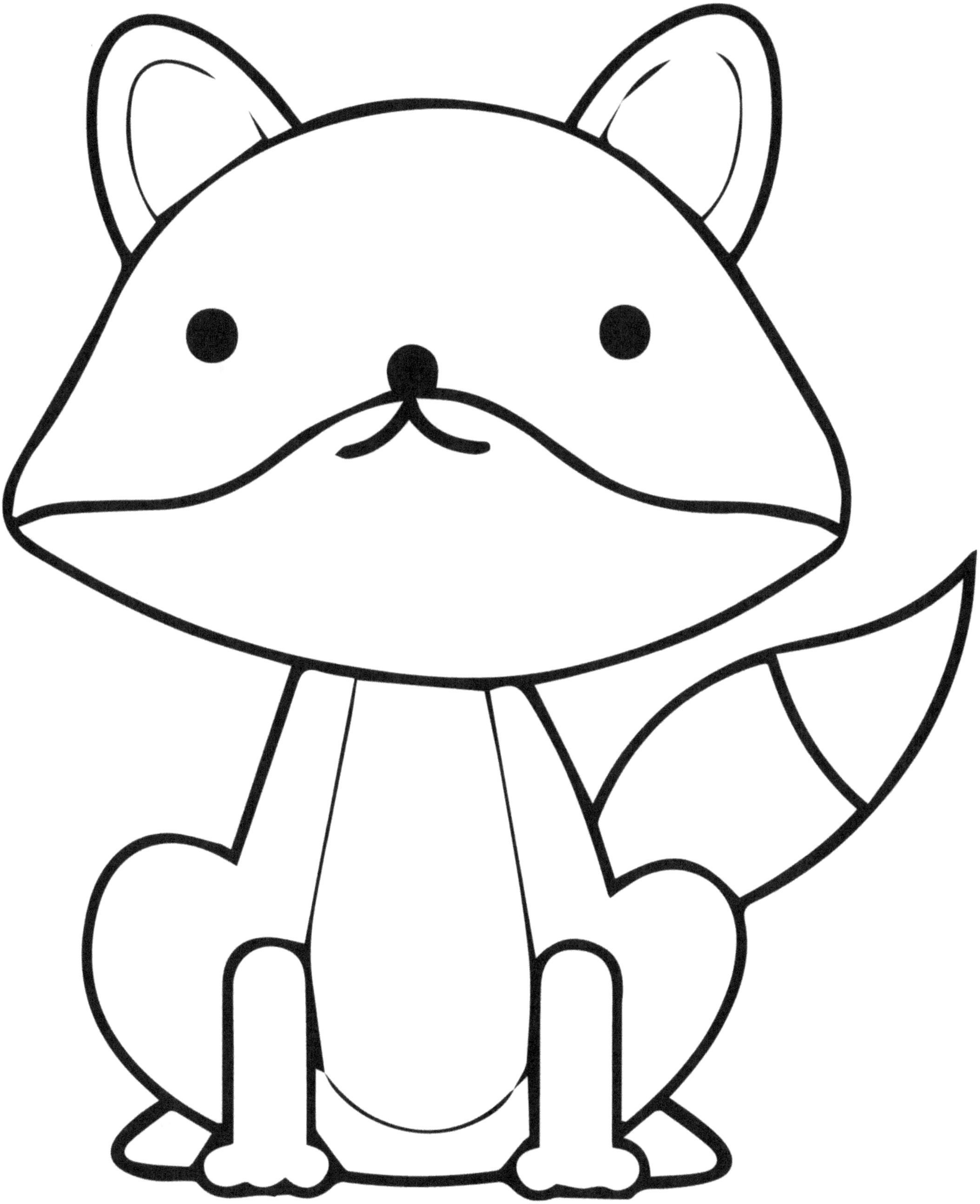

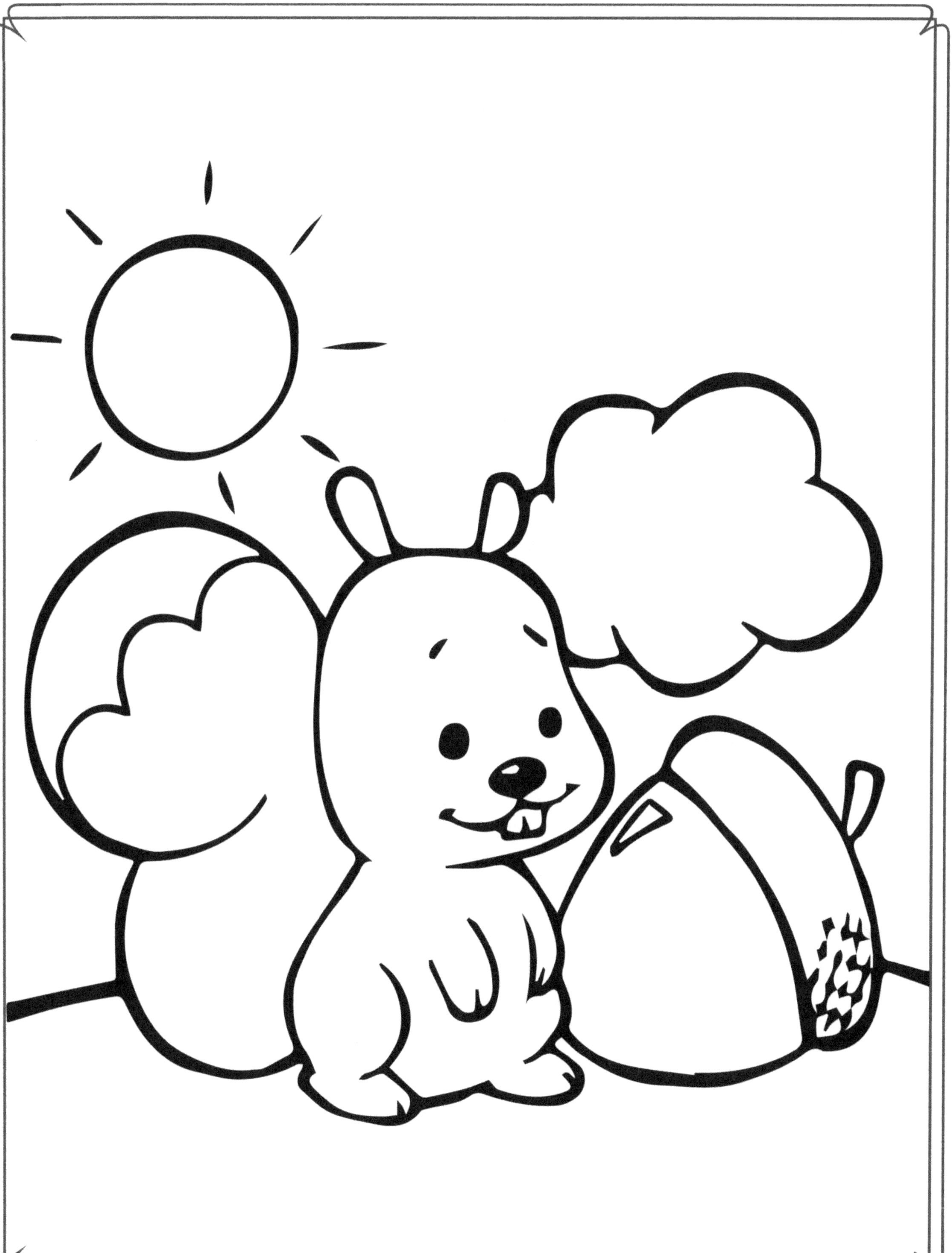

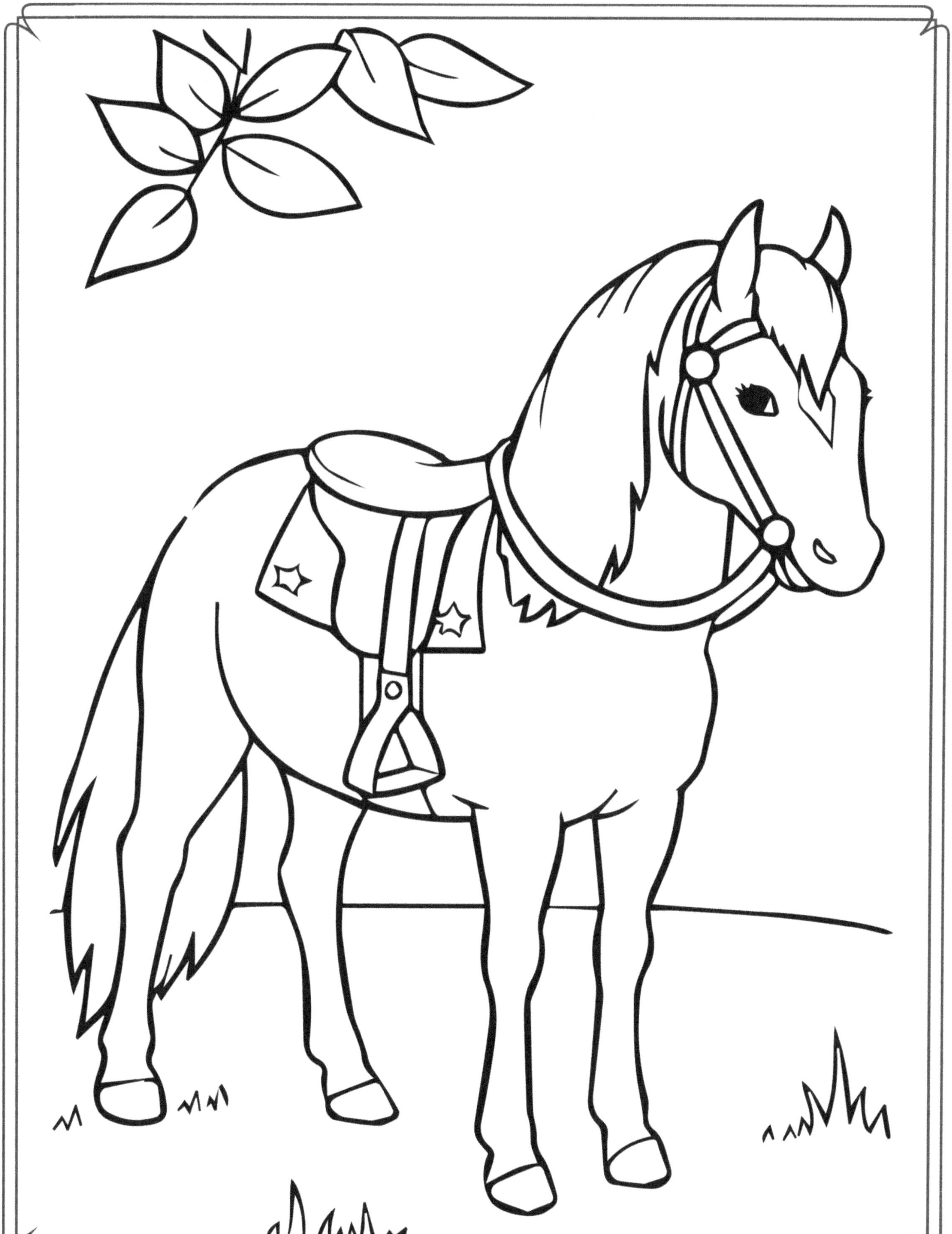

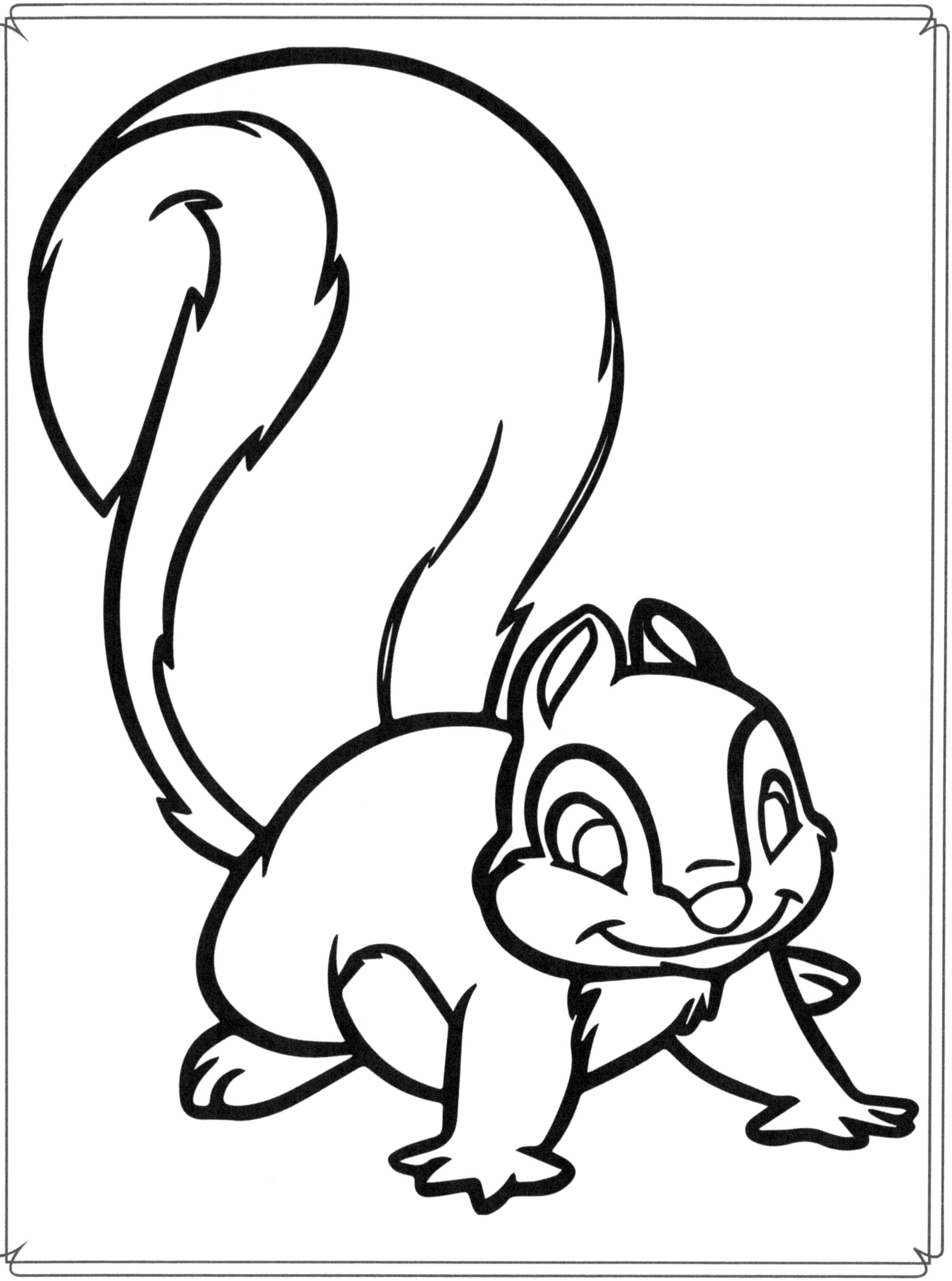

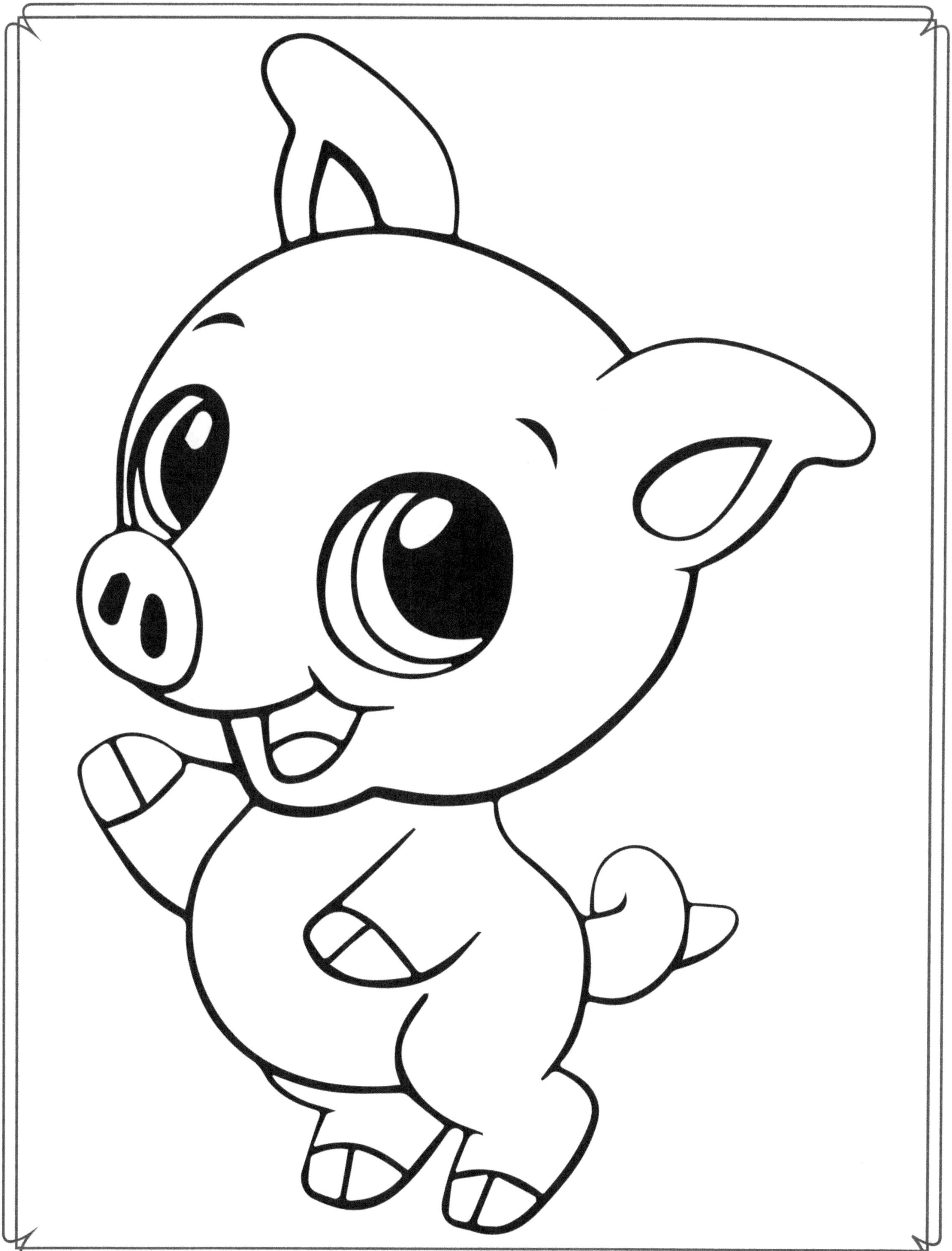

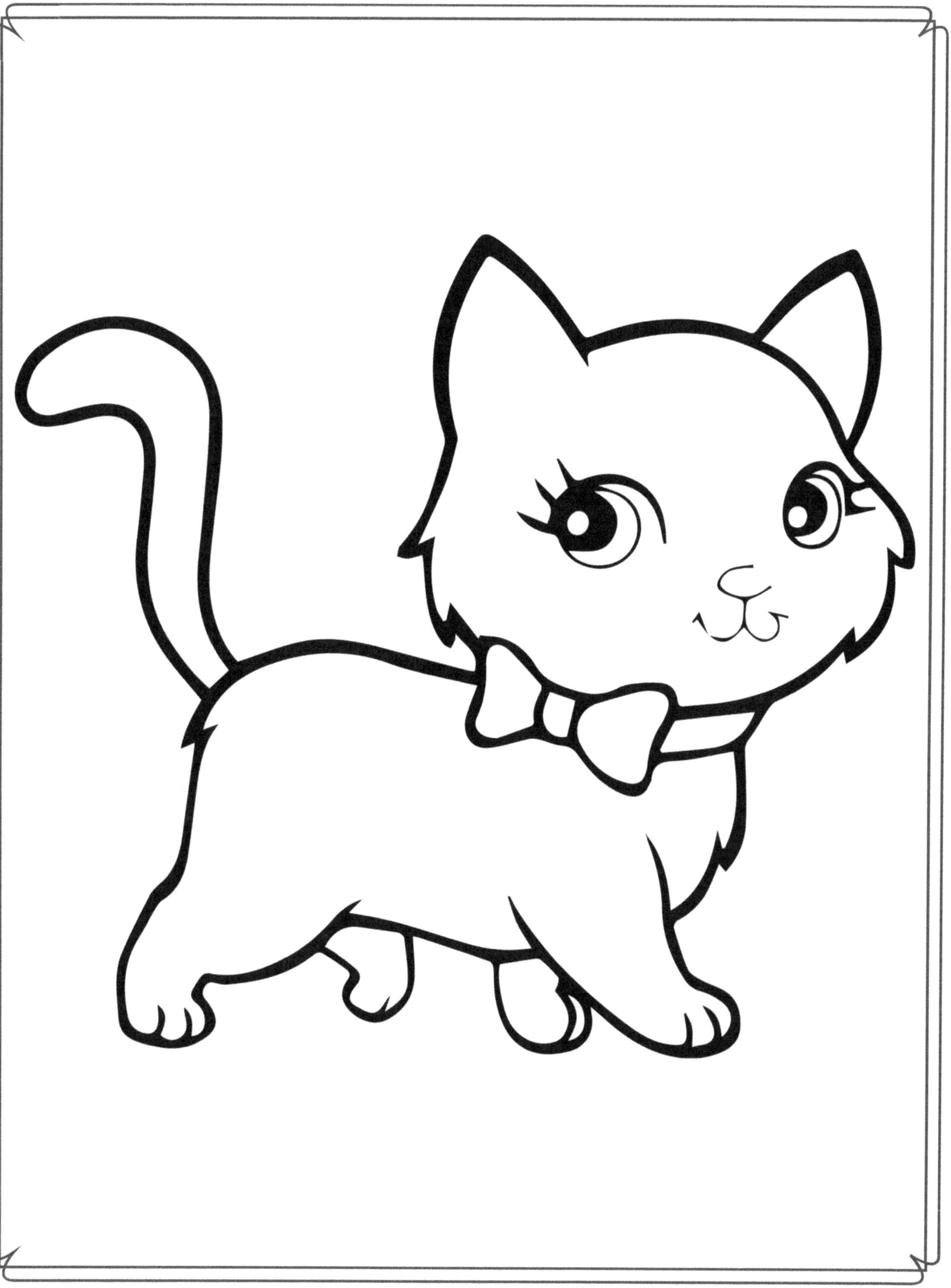

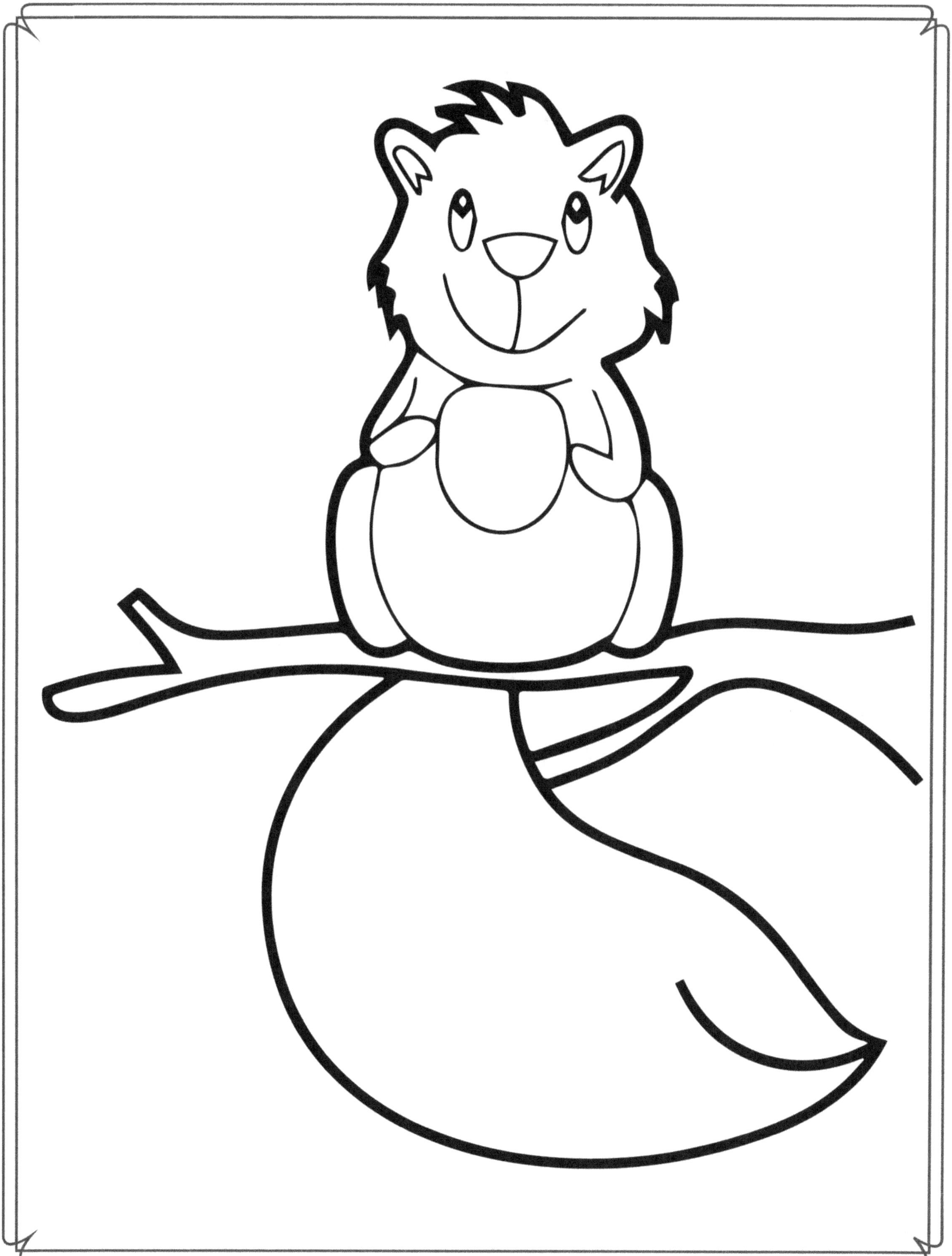

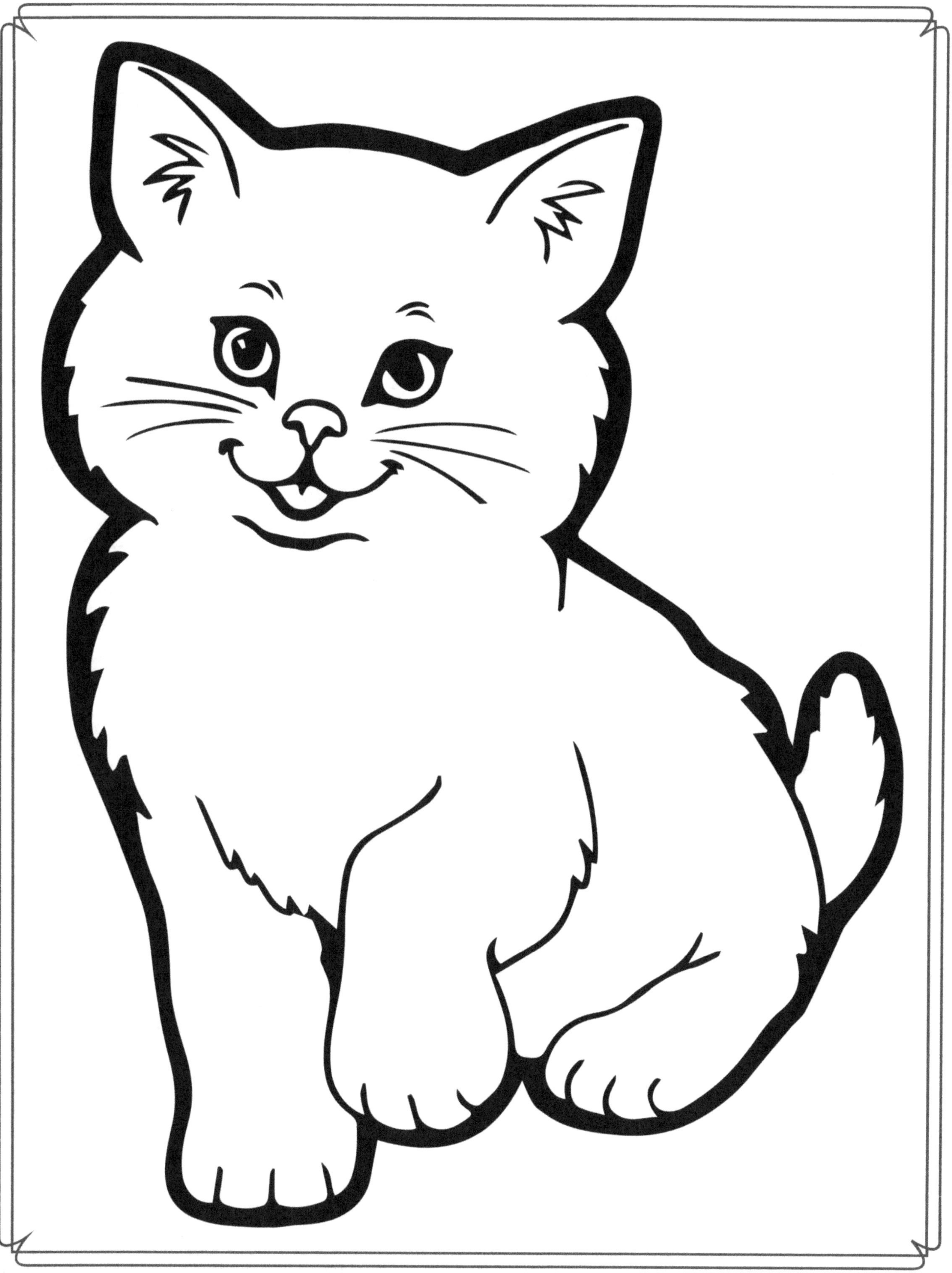

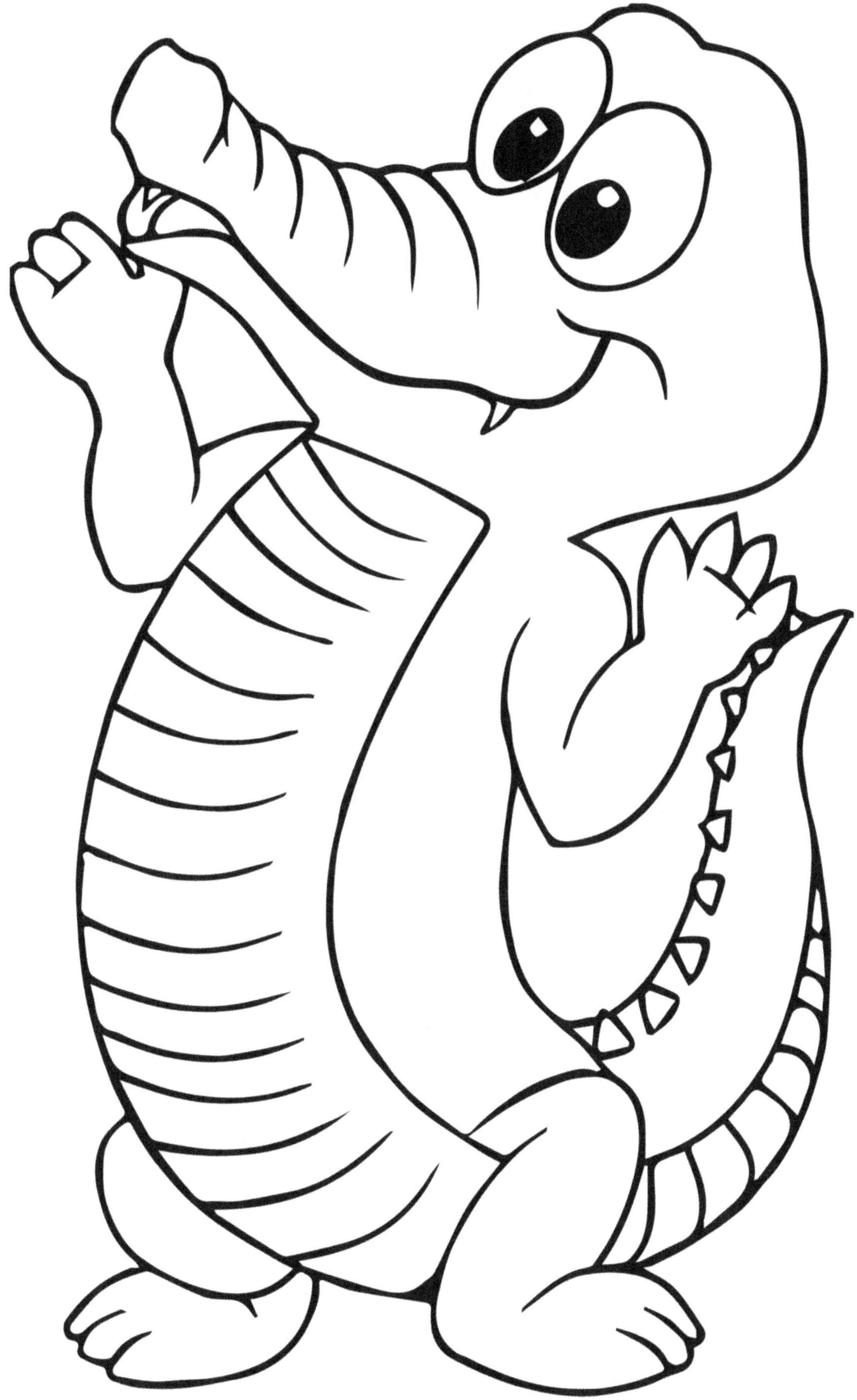

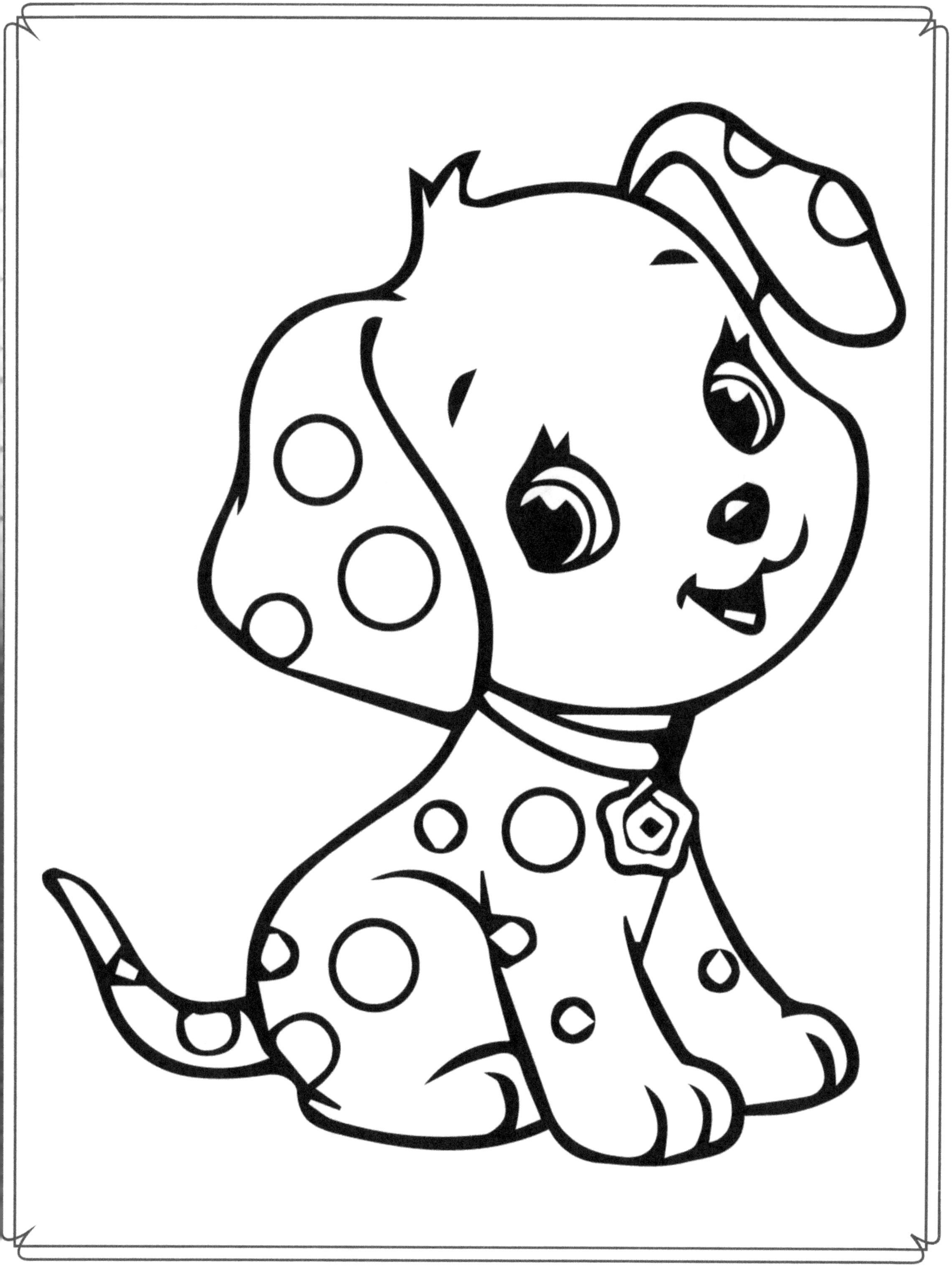

www.ingramcontent.com/pod-product-compliance
Lightning Source LLC
Chambersburg PA
CBHW081700220526
45466CB00009B/2832
9781676939719